LIFE COACHING
BULLET GUIDE

CW00727212

Bekki Hill

Hodder Education, 338 Euston Road, London NW1 3BH

Hodder Education is an Hachette UK company

First published in UK 2012 by Hodder Education

This edition published 2012

Artworks (internal and cover): Peter Lubach
Cover concept design: Two Associates

British Library Cataloguing in Publication Data: a catalogue record for this title is available from the British Library.

10 9 8 7 6 5 4 3 2 1

www.hoddereducation.co.uk

Typeset by Stephen Rowling/Springworks

Printed in Spain

Contents

Acknowledgements

A huge thank you to my husband, Steve, and my two amazing daughters for their love, support and inspiration. Thank you also to all the coaches, clients and friends who have challenged, supported and inspired me on my life-coaching journey.

About the author

Bekki Hill was so impressed by her own experience of life coaching that she trained to become a life coach. She qualified in May 2002 and began specializing in using life-coaching techniques to coach writers. As her experience grew, Bekki became a mentor and spent 3 years mentoring life-coaching students alongside running her own practice. Bekki is also a writer and has written many life-coaching-based features and articles. She has written a regular coaching column in writing magazine *Mslexia* since 2005, and in 2006 she wrote a coaching component for an MA in Screenwriting. She is the author of *Coach Yourself to Writing Success*, published by Hodder, Teach Yourself. For further information and Bekki's blog visit www.thewritecoach.co.uk. Follow Bekki on twitter @bekkiwritecoach.

Introduction

Life coaching enables people to make changes and to release their true potential in order that they live happier, more successful lives. Life coaches acknowledge that we are all individuals and the solutions which work for one person may not work for another. They operate in a non-directive manner – never telling, training, teaching or advising. Instead they use strong communication skills to enable their clients to:

* identify challenges
* find solutions
* establish what they want from the future
* set more achievable goals
* become more highly motivated
* think more creatively
* build stronger relationships
* become more positive
* discover and remove thinking patterns and beliefs that are holding them back
* develop greater confidence
* increase self-esteem
* maintain a coaching ethos within their life.

1 Designing a new life

If we are to live **happier, more successful** lives, we need to begin by considering how satisfied we are with the life we are currently living. This will enable us to identify what we want to add to our life, what we want to improve and what we want to remove.

Focusing clearly on what we truly desire can also save time and can reduce the stress we experience

Life coaching helps people redesign their lives by analysing:

* the balance they currently have within their lives
* how satisfied they are with their life
* what makes them happy
* what they want to achieve
* how they want to live their future life
* the realities of achieving what they desire
* the impact their desires will have on other people
* the sort of person they need to be to achieve their goals.

Go confidently in the direction of your dreams. Live the life you have imagined.

Henry David Thoreau

Life balance

The wheel of life allows us to create a visual representation of our current **life balance**.

To reflect on your satisfaction with the life you currently live, score on a 1–10 scale (10 = totally satisfied; 1 = totally dissatisfied) how happy you are with each life area identified on the wheel. When you do this, score how fulfilled you truly feel, not how content you think you ought to be with what you have.

Plotting your balance

Considering the centre of the wheel to be 0 and the edge of the wheel to be 10, plot your satisfaction scores on the wheel of life.

Shading in the inner wheel you have created will reflect **how smoothly your life is currently running**.

The wheel you create reveals both the current balance in your life and which areas you need to prioritize when making improvements.

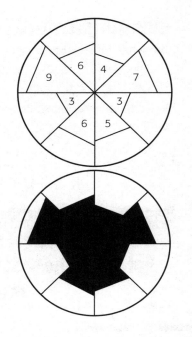

Creating a more fulfilling life

There are three ways we can make our lives more satisfying:

1 **Improve** what we already have.
2 **Add** new activities and goals to our lives.
3 **Remove** activities, situations or people that make us unhappy.

Brainstorming what we can **improve, remove or add** to a life area can identify changes we want to make that we might never have thought of otherwise. Once we have a list of possibilities, we can reflect on which changes we **really** want to make.

Researching and reflecting on all the possibilities that appeal to us can be time consuming, but this is the best way to ensure that our future is as fulfilling as we can make it

6

Future vision

Considering the future can help us discover more changes to make and establish **what we most desire**. Five ways to do this are:

1 Imagine you have died and complete the sentence, 'I wish I had …', 50 times.
2 Visualize where you want to be, what you will be doing and who you will be with 10 years from now.
3 Consider what you are putting off until you are older.
4 Ask, 'What must I achieve for my life to have been satisfying and well lived?'
5 Identify what you want to leave behind for others.

The realities of our dreams

When we design our future it's important to ensure that it's what we really want. This can be done by asking the following questions:

* Are we **settling** for what we think we can have, rather than aiming for what we really want?
* Are we chasing any achievements because someone **expects** us to achieve them?
* Are we attempting to **compete** with friends or siblings?
* Have we **outgrown** our need to achieve a certain dream?
* Are we **running away** from something and chasing a particular goal because it appears to be an escape route?

Consequences

Everything we do impacts on our lives and the lives of those around us.
We should always check the consequences of making any changes by
considering:

* what we will lose
* what we will gain
* what impact the change
  will have on others
* how we will spend our time
* how much it will cost
* if we are truly happy to
  make the change.

I think I need a new career.

● Always consider the impact your choices will have on others

Creating a new you

To achieve the life we want to live, we need to be the sort of person who takes the sort of actions that will achieve our desires. Therefore, when you design your life, you also need to **consider whether there are any attributes you need to improve or acquire**, such as:

- personal qualities
- different ways of behaving
- new skills.

For anything you want to accomplish always ask:

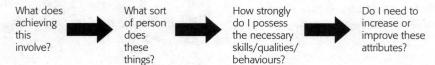

What does achieving this involve? → What sort of person does these things? → How strongly do I possess the necessary skills/qualities/behaviours? → Do I need to increase or improve these attributes?

CASE STUDY

When 27-year-old Mandy considered her wheel of life, she identified that she was unhappy with her:

* career in the pharmaceutical industry
* finances
* lack of personal development.

By considering her career as priority and reflecting on her choices – both past and future – Mandy realized that she had taken a chemistry degree to please her parents; however, she disliked working in a laboratory. Mandy decided to study for a marketing qualification and seek a marketing job within the pharmaceutical industry. This addressed her lack of career satisfaction and personal development. In the long term this should also improve her finances.

2 Goal setting

Once we have identified something we want to gain or achieve, coaching encourages us to view it as a goal. **A goal is basically a target to aim for.** How we set that target and how we plan to achieve it can have a huge impact on what we finally accomplish.

Without a target to aim for it is easy to lose focus on what we want to achieve

When we set a goal we need to:

* identify exactly what we want to accomplish
* decide how long we expect to take to achieve it
* phrase our goal so that it is more easily accomplished
* define the steps we need to take to achieve it
* ensure that our goal and our plans to realize it are realistic and achievable
* work on achieving the goal!

● We all need a target to aim for

Defining your target

We need to know exactly what we want to accomplish in order to:

* identify the best steps to take to achieve it
* focus fully and accurately on accomplishing it
* recognize when we have achieved it.

Finding ways of measuring some goals will be easy, but it will be harder for others. For example, a weight loss target is easy to define. However, there is no immediately obvious way to measure a goal to become more confident.

Useful questions to ask if you **struggle to place measures** on defining what you want to accomplish are:

* What will I be **able to do** when I have achieved this?
* What will I **see, hear** and **feel** when I have reached this goal?
* What will other people **notice** is different about me?
* What will I **have** when I've accomplished this goal that I don't have now?
* How will my life have **improved** when I achieve this?

No wind serves him who addresses his voyage to no certain port.

Michel de Montaigne

Creating a goal

The way goals are phrased is very important. Goals need to be personal, precise, present tense and positive:

Personal	The goal must be important to the person who is achieving it
Precise	Goals state exactly what we will achieve and when we will achieve it
Present tense	Writing a goal in the present tense allows our subconscious to see the goal as 'happening' now. This encourages us to work on it and not put it off until later
Positive	Negative statements (*for example saying that we will lose a certain amount of weight*) are unattractive to our subconscious, and therefore we will be less highly motivated to achieve them

18

Examples of goals that are precise, personal, positive and present tense are:

> 'I will be a romantic novelist publishing one book a year by my 50th birthday.'

> 'I will weigh 9 stone 10 pounds by 31 July this year.'

Writing our goals down helps us to **remember to work on them** and enables us to **focus** on them **more clearly**. Places it can be helpful to write your goals down are:

* in a goal journal
* inside your wardrobe door
* above your computer
* on an achievement card in your wallet or diary.

A goal properly set is halfway reached.

Abraham Lincoln

Breaking goals down

Coaching breaks goals into:

1 long-term goals
2 medium-term goals
3 short-term goals.

It's easy to put off working towards a goal or lose focus on a goal if we see it as something we won't achieve for a very long time. Long-term goals may also seem so big that accomplishing them feels impossible or highly unlikely and we therefore don't even start working towards them.

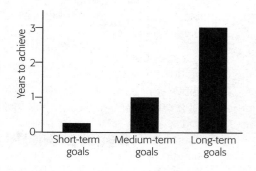

20

To make goals more achievable coaching:

* breaks long-term goals into medium- and short-term goals that lead to achieving the long-term goal
* breaks medium-term goals into short-term goals that lead to achieving the medium-term goal.

For example, the long-term goal, 'I will have written a novel in 3 years' time' could be broken into:

Year 1

* Medium-term: attend a year-long writing course.
* Short-term: sign up for course and attend weekly.

Year 2

* Medium-term: complete first draft by the end of this year.
* Short-term: write two chapters a month.

Year 3

* Medium-term: complete novel by the end of this year.
* Short-term: edit/rewrite one chapter a week.

Action plans

Once long- and medium-term goals have been broken into short-term goals, coaching focuses on creating **action plans** to achieve each short-term goal by:

1 identifying the steps we need to take in the next **3 months** to achieve it
2 defining exactly **when we will take each step** and what we will do.

Once we have defined a goal and an associated action plan, we need to take the appropriate actions at the appropriate times.

Plans to achieve goals need to be realistic and achievable. However, if you have done your best to achieve a goal, don't be hard on yourself if it takes longer to accomplish than intended

CASE STUDY

Fifty-year-old Lucy's goal required her to lose 42 pounds in 18 months. Her short-term action plan was:

Week 1

* Visit nurse and discuss healthy weight loss.
* Identify suitable exercise in line with nurse's advice.

Week 2

* Start eating healthily.
* Start exercising.
* Ask friends for support and encouragement.

Weeks 3–13

* Follow exercise and healthy eating programmes.
* Weigh myself once a week.

Once Lucy had gained advice from the nurse, she added what she would eat and her exercise programme to her plan.

3 Beliefs

A belief is what we hold to be true, whether it is or not. Life coaching helps us to identify and reduce the influence of beliefs that limit us and hold us back. It also helps us form new, more constructive beliefs.

Beliefs are not in themselves good or bad, but the impact they have on us can determine whether or not we achieve our goals and life ambitions

By exploring and working on our beliefs we can:

* recognize the impact that our beliefs have on us
* identify beliefs that limit us
* understand why we are holding back in certain areas
* remove beliefs that limit us
* achieve our goals more easily
* create beliefs that inspire and motivate
* recognize unhelpful thinking patterns
* increase our general positivity.

Nothing can stop the man with the right mental attitude from achieving his goal; nothing on earth can help the man with the wrong mental attitude.

Thomas Jefferson

The impact of our beliefs

We all have an internal dialogue within our thoughts in which we:

1 discuss things with ourselves
2 relive memories
3 cheer ourselves on
4 express fear and negativity.

This internal voice learns what it knows from our life experiences.

Experience ➡ Memory created ➡ Memory recalled when we anticipate or encounter a similar experience

When our minds throw up fearful thoughts, we become anxious and often avoid doing whatever those thoughts are warning us about

If we've had a **negative experience** in the past, this is likely to generate negativity and fear about repeating the experience or a similar experience.

Negative experience ➡ Fearful/ negative memories ➡ Avoid repeating negative experience or experiences we perceive to be similar

If we've had a **positive experience** in the past, this will generate positivity towards repeating the experience or a similar experience.

Positive experience ➡ Positive memories ➡ Happy to repeat positive experience or experiences we perceive to be similar

Identifying limiting thinking

A life coach assists their clients to recognize:

1 the **reasons** they believe they can't do or achieve something
2 the **attitude** that they have towards their challenges
3 **thinking patterns** that may give clues to subconscious reasons they are stuck or struggling to achieve something
4 **fears** that they hold about taking certain actions, achieving something or stepping out of a comfort zone
5 things that they believe they **should** be doing, but don't really want to.

TOP TIP
In reality few things are truly impossible – we just haven't recognized a solution yet or we don't like the solution we see.

When a coach hears a client express limiting thinking, they will raise it in the client's awareness using skilful questioning. This usually leads to uncovering one of the following three situations:

1 The client is **anxious** about doing something because they are afraid to step out of a comfort zone.
2 The client **doesn't really want to** do what they thought they wanted to do.
3 The client holds **limiting beliefs** that prevent them accomplishing what they want to achieve.

Changing beliefs

When we identify and explore our limiting beliefs, we may find that **some beliefs limit our behaviour for good reasons**: for example, *preventing us from taking an unacceptably high financial risk*. However, we will also find beliefs that are holding us back which we want to change or remove.

32

We may recognize that some beliefs are *old thinking patterns* that don't apply to us today, or we may simply be anxious about doing something because it is new. Becoming consciously aware of these sorts of thoughts may be all that is needed for us to let go of them. However, other beliefs may need further work.

The following steps can be used to remove or change more deeply seated beliefs:

1 Identify a new belief that you want to hold that contradicts the limiting belief.
2 Gather evidence that contradicts the limiting belief.
3 Take action to prove that the limiting belief is wrong and the new belief you want to adopt is true.

The best place to **find evidence to contradict limiting beliefs** is in our own past. This allows us to recognize that the limiting belief isn't always true. If there is no evidence in our past, reflection on the reasons why other people don't hold the limiting belief can help us recognize that we don't have to act consistently with it.

Thinking patterns

As well as beliefs associated with specific challenges, we hold beliefs that form thinking patterns that permeate our general approach to life. For example:

Thinking patterns that limit us:

* I'm an unlucky person.
* I am who I am.
* I'm stupid.
* I always get things wrong.

Thinking patterns that liberate us:

* I'm lucky.
* I can do anything I put my mind to.
* I'm clever.
* I'm always right.

CASE STUDY

Eli avoided crowds because they made her anxious. She identified the limiting belief, 'something bad will happen', had developed from her experience as a child prone to fainting in crowded places.

Eli eroded her limiting belief by:

* refusing to avoid crowded places
* reminding herself that nothing bad had ever happened to her in a crowded place.

Over time Eli's belief faded.

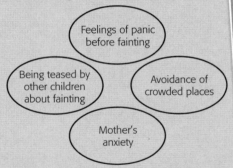

4 Values

Our core values are **fundamental principles** that are important to us. They have a strong pull on our emotions and desires and therefore **influence our decisions, focus and motivation, what stresses us and, ultimately, what we achieve**. They are identified by simple descriptors such as respect, honesty, support, simplicity, creativity, individuality, loyalty …

Our values are our own personal set of rules by which we live our lives

By defining ourselves in a simple word portrait of our core values we can:

* recognize why we become stressed in particular situations
* create goals that are likely to be truly satisfying when we achieve them
* understand the reasons we are motivated in some situations and not in others
* build greater motivation to accomplish our ambitions
* simplify some of our decision making
* understand the roots of our conflicts more easily.

He who knows others is wise; he who knows himself is enlightened.

Lao-Tzu

Identifying core values

We all have a unique set of values that is reflected in the choices we make. By examining the life we are currently living, we can identify our core values.

Uncovering your core values

Make a list of:

* the things you own that are important to you
* activities you choose to spend your free time on
* activities you would like to spend your free time on, but are currently unable to
* places you choose to go regularly
* places you have really enjoyed being
* who you enjoy spending time with and what you value most about your relationship with them.

Once you have a list, for each item ask yourself, 'What's important to me about this?'. **Keep asking this question of each answer you identify** until you have one or more simple descriptors of values that you recognize as being important to you.

CASE STUDY

Astrid identified the things she loved about dancing as:

* fun
* creativity

* sharing
* exercise.

Fun, creativity and sharing are simple descriptors and therefore values. Exercise is not – so Astrid asked what was important about exercise. Her answer was health. Health is not a simple descriptor, so she asked what was important about health. Her answer was freedom. Freedom is a simple descriptor and therefore a value.

Values and goals

Because our values have a strong influence on our emotions and desires, **goals that link to our values are more achievable and more fulfilling** when we accomplish them.

Goal linked to one or more values	STRONG MOTIVATION	Satisfaction achieved by fulfilling values when goal is realised
Goal **NOT** linked to any values	Weak or no motivation	Lack of satisfaction if goal is realised

Although our values are fairly stable, they can change, especially if we experience life-changing events or something that shifts our perspective significantly

If we have a goal that doesn't satisfy our values, we need to consider:

1 Whether we really want to achieve it.
2 Does the goal facilitate another goal that satisfies our values? If this is the case, we can increase motivation by reminding ourselves that it is a stepping stone to the second goal.
3 If our values have changed and we need to reconsider all our goals.

TOP TIP
Linking your activities to as many values as possible can boost motivation. For example, a value of connection could be satisfied by doing research by interviewing people instead of researching documents.

Values and stress

When our values are **confronted** or **dishonoured** we become stressed, upset or even angry. For example, if we value reliability, we may get annoyed if people don't turn up on time.

Understanding our values can help us to recognize that we are experiencing a particular reaction because a value is being confronted or dishonoured. This allows us to accept and experience our emotions more easily, rather than burying them, denying them or becoming consumed by them.

Knowing that different people hold different core values also helps us to understand that people who upset us are unlikely to be upsetting us intentionally; they just don't share the same values as us.

Looking ahead

Recognizing how our values influence our behaviour enables us to predict when stress or conflict may occur and take action:

1 We can work to **prevent** conflict arising.
2 If we recognize that conflict is inevitable, or very likely, we can **prepare** ourselves and identify how we can act to our best advantage.

TOP TIP
In general we tend to get on better with people whose values are closely aligned to our own.

Upholding our values

Some of our values are specific to certain life areas, and sometimes **values held in different life areas can come into conflict**.

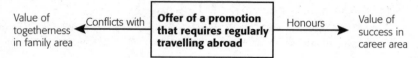

| Value of togetherness in family area | ←Conflicts with | **Offer of a promotion that requires regularly travelling abroad** | Honours→ | Value of success in career area |

Our values usually fall into a natural hierarchy, so normally the value that we prize most highly wins out. However, we are likely to experience inner conflict:

1 while deciding between the choices attached to these values
2 afterwards, as the value that is lost continues to be confronted by the choice we have made.

Confidence

Because our identity is closely linked to our values, we can lose confidence when:

Other people

* Keep acting against our values.
* Continually tell us our values aren't important.

We

* Keep giving in to other people's choices.
* Fail to go with our gut feeling and act to please others.

As *our values define who we are*, if we are fighting against them, or denying any of them, we're rejecting that part of ourselves. Understanding and honouring our values is therefore essential in building self-esteem and learning to love and accept ourselves.

5 Confidence and self-esteem

If we have low self-esteem we place little **value** or **trust** in who we are or what we do and consequently lack confidence. However, we may have high self-esteem and still lack confidence in a particular situation.

If we are to live happy, successful lives, we need to be comfortable with the person we are and act with confidence

When working with a client, a life coach may hear them make negative statements about themselves and what they believe they cannot do. These **limiting beliefs** may be overcome by raising them in the client's awareness and creating or collecting evidence against them. However, further tools may also be needed.

Key tools that can help eliminate beliefs that undermine confidence and self-esteem are:

* building positive self-attitude
* affirmations
* metaphors
* visualization.

If you put small value on yourself, rest assured that the world will not raise your price.

Anonymous

Attitude

Low self-esteem and lack of confidence can be displayed as reticent behaviour and/or verbal negativity. However, sometimes people appear positive, but silently or subconsciously question themselves and their abilities. This often results in them being **overly self-conscious or forceful** in their actions and/or communication.

A skilful coach will recognize negative self-attitude in a client and encourage them to explore it, whether the client recognizes it themself or not.

In order for us to address the beliefs that undermine our self-esteem, we need to be prepared to acknowledge that we hold negativity about ourselves

52

We can build positive self-attitude by using the following process:

STEP ONE
Choose to be more aware of our thoughts about ourselves and what we say

STEP TWO
When we recognise negative self-attitude or self-doubt, consider what could be positive about this. For example the thought, 'I am shy', could be seen as 'I like to get a measure of people before I trust them.'

STEP THREE
Every time we hear ourselves thinking the undermining thought, remind ourselves of the positive related to it and refuse to think that thought again

Affirmations

Thoughts are carried within our brains along physical pathways. When we think a particular thought the pathways carrying it become stronger, making it easier for us to have that thought again. Therefore, **the more often we think positively about ourselves, the easier it becomes** to think positively and be positive about ourselves.

An affirmation is a phrase that tells us something positive about:

* who we are
* what we do

* what we can do
* what we have.

If we **repeat** an affirmation to ourselves a hundred times a day, it will grow the pathway that carries it through our brain and help us build a new, more positive attitude.

- ☑ Deciding on a **time** of day to repeat our affirmations can help us ensure that we remember to work on them.
- ☑ If we struggle to believe an affirmation, saying 'I can …', 'I am learning to …', 'I am improving …' or something similar, rather than 'I am', will make it more believable.
- ☑ Saying an affirmation **out loud** while we look in the mirror will increase the impact it has on us.

Metaphors

Metaphors allow us to express and give form to **complex feelings, behaviours, situations and ideas**, which we would otherwise find difficult or impossible to explain. They therefore enable us to:

* understand and express more clearly how we feel
* connect more strongly to our doubts and fears linked to low self-esteem and lack of confidence
* communicate more effectively with our subconscious.

Creating and replaying a metaphor that changes a negative self-image into a positive one can be used to build and reinforce confidence and self-esteem.

When there is no enemy within, the enemies outside cannot hurt you.

African Proverb

Metaphors to build confidence and self-esteem can be created using the following process:

1 Identify the undermining thought: for example, 'Nobody cares about my opinion.'
2 Write down how this makes you feel: for example insignificant, unimportant, invisible …
3 Identify the word that you consider most appropriate for how you feel.
4 Close your eyes and imagine how you look when you are being that word. Perhaps you look like a mouse when you are insignificant, or a screwed up piece of paper if you're unimportant.
5 Change the picture so it gradually becomes more positive. For example, the mouse could morph into a tiger.

Visualization

Repeatedly visualizing metaphors or imagining ourselves behaving more positively in daunting situations are good ways to build confidence and self-esteem. However, we can make our visualization **more effective by engaging all our senses and feelings**.

Hearing
What will people say?
What sounds will you hear?
Play relaxing or invigorating music as you visualize

Touch
What will you touch?
What might be touching you?

Sight
What will you see?

Smell
What might you smell?

Feelings
Imagine what you will feel when you achieve your goal

Taste
What might you taste?

When performing a visualization:

1 Relax.
2 Close your eyes.
3 Take sufficient time to really explore it.
4 Allow it to grow and become even more positive than before.

CASE STUDY

As part of her plan to overcome her nerves about public speaking
Samira created a visualization of:

* herself speaking in a calm, collected manner, dressed in the
  clothes she planned to wear
* the audience smiling as she spoke and cheering as she finished
* people patting her on the shoulder and telling her how great her
  speech had been
* herself sipping champagne afterwards to celebrate.

6 Relationships

It is impossible to function rationally in the world without having relationships with other people. Good relationships are not only **essential for a harmonious life**, they are also **key to living a successful life**. Life coaching assists us to address difficult and detrimental relationships and develop those that nourish and support us.

Healthy relationships are mutually beneficial to everyone involved

We all have a huge impact on each other's lives, and improving our relationships may be a topic that we recognize we need to address. However, even if we do not, life coaching often leads us to consider our relationships within the context of exploring our lives and working towards our goals. Areas that frequently need to be considered are:

* who is supporting us
* the level of support we have
* unsupportive relationships
* the boundaries we create for others.

A doubtful friend is worse than a certain enemy.

Aesop

Supportive relationships

When we look for support, it's usually for practical help with physical challenges, to reduce our workload or to save time. However, **psychological support** is just as important to our **success** and **well-being**, yet we rarely consciously seek it out.

People who support us are those whose words and actions are supportive of:

* us
* our abilities
* our goals
* the other people we want in our lives
* our possessions.

When a life coach assists a client to create a plan, they will ask the client questions such as:

> Who supports you?

> Do you need more practical support?

> Do you need more psychological support?

> Who/what works against you achieving your goals?

If necessary the coach will then encourage the client to:

* **increase** the level of **support** they have
* consider **those who are undermining them** in greater detail.

Unsupportive relationships

Anyone who **unnecessarily takes up your time**, oversteps your boundaries or **undermines you** will have a **negative impact** on your happiness and what you achieve. They may also cause you stress.

The people who most frequently sabotage us rarely mean to do so. They are usually our friends and family and, even when they undermine us, they do it because they:

* think they're being supportive
* don't realise they're doing it
* have their own agenda.

The four types of people who most commonly sabotage us

People we support	The people we care about most can have the biggest negative impact on us. Of course it's crucial that we support them, but, because we love them, we sometimes we get our priorities confused
People who are negative	People who have a generally negative attitude and people who believe that we can't achieve certain things in particular tend to erode our self-belief and positivity
People who interrupt us	In a world where communication is so simple, it's easy to allow all manner of people to interrupt and take up our attention away from our goals
Vampires	Some people take from us (intentionally and unintentionally) without ever giving something back

Addressing your boundaries

1 People you support

It's easy to assume roles or fall into patterns of behaviour within close relationships.

Good questions to ask when we consider the support we give others are:

* What are my priorities?
* Am I doing all the giving?
* Am I doing this because I always have?
* Do I want to keep doing this?
* Am I really helping them by doing this?

2 Negativity

When people are excessively negative consider how you can:

* reduce their negative impact
* help them to become more positive.

It is important to remember that it is not the relationship itself that is unsupportive, but the boundaries that currently exist within that relationship

68

3 Interruption

For people who cause interruption consider:

* what boundaries you need to set
* how to explain these boundaries and the reasons you need them.

For interruption from communications consider:

* your priorities and whether you need to respond so quickly
* how to minimize gadgets grabbing your attention unnecessarily.

4 Vampires

If people take without giving, consider:

* the reasons you allow them into your life
* if you really want them to remain in your life
* how you can reduce their negative impact
* if it's time you made some new friends.

Addressing unsupportive behaviour

If we continue to accept or forgive someone's behaviour, he or she is likely to continue to behave that way. It is only by **refusing to accept** someone's behaviour that we can break the cycle.

Unsupportive behaviour

Allowing the behaviour gives out the message that it is acceptable

We allow the behaviour

Relationships are important and complex. Any time we consider making changes within a relationship, we need to explore:

* the possible consequences of taking action to make the change
* the possible consequences of not addressing that change.

CASE STUDY

After Liz's mother suffered a heart attack, she kept making excuses to call Liz over to her house because she was afraid of being taken ill again when she was alone. Liz felt compelled to respond, because she was scared that, if she didn't, her mother would work herself up into having another heart attack.

Coaching helped Liz realize that she could take control. She created a plan to move in with her mother then leave her alone for increasing amounts of time.

Three months later, Liz moved back out and gave a key to a neighbour for emergencies. Liz was reclaiming her life and no longer worrying about or getting angry with her mother.

7 Living the best life you can

Life coaching isn't a quick fix. To live the best life we can, we need to maintain an ongoing process of **self-awareness** and taking **responsibility** for our lives and the impact we have on others.

Maintaining good practices is key to ensuring that we reap the benefits of the plans we create and the discoveries we make about ourselves during life coaching

As time progresses we change, our plans change and the world around us changes. However, simple tools and reminders can be used to sustain and build on the benefits initially achieved by life coaching. These tools allow us to:

* keep focused on our goals and priorities and make adjustments when necessary
* ensure continued commitment to our goals
* preserve a realistic life balance
* make success more achievable.

It is not the strongest of the species that survives, nor the most intelligent; it is the one that is most adaptable to change.

Charles Darwin

Reviewing goals

When we set goals it is essential to regularly review them to ensure that we:

* stay on track
* take into consideration any changes that have taken place since we set them.

Carrying out reviews weekly, 3 monthly, 6 monthly and yearly allows us to:

* keep track of our progress
* create regular plans
* assess our progress
* create short-term goals from medium- and long-term goals we previously identified and create medium-term goals from long-term goals
* create new goals
* adjust our goals when necessary.

Useful questions to ask when we review our goals are:

What have I achieved since the last review?
What have I learned?
What will I do differently in future because of what I have learned?

Do I need to adjust my goals or action plans?
What do I want/need to achieve before the next review?
Are there any goals I want to add, remove or modify?

How have I grown/changed?

What didn't work out as I planned?
What can I do differently to get the result I was looking for?

What obstacles have I overcome?
What obstacles might I face in the future?

Commitment

Checking our commitment when we set a goal, when we review it or when we feel our motivation flagging:

* allows us to measure how likely we are to achieve that goal
* gives us opportunity **to boost our motivation** to accomplish it.

We can check our commitment by scoring on a scale of 1–10 how committed we are to achieving a goal or task related to it.

☑ 10 = absolutely sure we're going to do it.
☒ 1 = we're definitely not going to do it.

Score	Meaning
10	We're fully committed
7–9	We need to ask ourselves what we can do to increase our commitment. It shouldn't be a problem if we can't raise our score, but it's always good to ensure that our motivation is as strong as possible
6 or below	If we score below 7, we're unlikely to find the motivation to complete the action(s) in question. We therefore need to ask what we can do to increase our commitment. Once we have found a way, we need to rescore our commitment. If it is still less than 7, we need to consider whether we really want to achieve the goal in question

Balance

When we set goals and become excited by them, it can be easy to spend the majority of our time focused on what we want to achieve in the future. We can fail to create happy successful lives, because we forget to **maintain our health or enjoy the here and now**.

In reality balance is almost impossible to achieve as there is always likely to be something that needs a greater amount of our attention. We therefore need to be **constantly aware of our equilibrium** and ensure that we are **heading towards balance** rather than away from it.

When we relax, have fun or take part in new experiences, we need to engage as fully as possible, thus ensuring that we are living in the present moment with the experience

Working towards balance means ensuring that we:

* give attention to all of our
  life areas and our goals
  associated with them
* remove mental and physical
  clutter as it arises
* give appropriate attention to
  tasks according to their priority
* take time to relax, have
  fun and take part in new
  experiences
* are taking action rather than
  reacting to time pressures.

Making success more achievable

Life coaching also offers tools that help maintain focus and boost motivation by reminding us of our goals and the life that we are creating. They include:

1 **treasure maps** – created by making a collage of pictures of what we want to have and to achieve
2 **visualizing** ourselves achieving our goals
3 **affirmations** that describe a future achievement
4 **collections** of items that remind us what we have already achieved
5 **timelines** depicting what we have achieved and what we need to achieve towards a specific goal.

Celebrating success

It is important to celebrate both achieving **minor milestones** and **completing our goals**. By doing this we:

* acknowledge our achievement
* gain greater fulfilment
* raise our positivity
* boost our motivation to be more successful.

CASE STUDY

Once Chang had finished working with his life coach, he continued to regularly review his goals and commitment to them. Although he often found his life becoming quite hectic, he set aside time in his diary to relax and enjoy himself.

Chang also created and used a treasure map of everything he wanted in his life to ensure that he kept focused on all his dreams and ambitions.

8 The coaching process

A coaching session creates a space in which the **client can explore their challenges** in a completely non-judgemental, non-directive environment. Although this is a fluid process, it tends to follow a general pattern of:

1 reviewing previous progress
2 exploring a specific challenge
3 establishing how the client plans to move forward.

Each coaching session focuses entirely on the client and his or her needs, wants and desires
....

A life coaching interaction can be described as consisting of five stages:

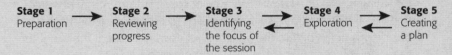

Although a coaching interaction generally moves in the direction of stage 5, *creating a plan,* there can be movement back and forth between stages 3, 4 and 5.

The unexamined life is not worth living.

Socrates

Stage 1: Preparation

The coach's preparation

Coaching needs to take place in a quiet space with **minimal** physical and visual **distractions**. The coach needs to refamiliarize themself with the client's notes before the session, but does not expect the client to focus on any particular subject within the session.

The coach also needs to spend approximately 15 minutes immediately prior to each session clearing their own thoughts and emotions. If they do not, it will be impossible to listen properly and focus fully on the client's needs.

TOP TIP

Good ways to clear space:

* meditation
* listening to music
* repeating a mantra.

Client preparation

Prior to a coaching session the coach may offer a **worksheet for the client to complete**. This is likely to be:

* a questionnaire provided at the start of the coaching relationship to help establish what the client hopes to gain from the coaching, *or*
* a simple questionnaire to focus the client on what they have achieved since the previous session and what they want to consider in the coming session.

Many coaches do not provide questionnaires beyond initial assessment. However, it is still important for clients to come to each session aware of the area or challenge they wish to discuss.

Stage 2: Reviewing progress

Apart from the first session, each coaching session begins by reviewing the progress the client has made since the previous session. Here the coach will:

- ☑ congratulate the client on progress made
- ☑ remain non-judgemental about what the client has not achieved.

Although the coach never judges the client, he or she is responsible for holding them accountable for their actions and inactions between sessions. However, the coach must not allow these discussions to overwhelm a session if the client wishes to discuss a different matter.

Stage 3: Identifying the session focus

Sometimes a client knows exactly what they want to get out of the session. Other times they:

* initially seem sure but change their mind
* only have a vague idea
* are completely unsure
* know what they want to discuss, but are reluctant to speak about it.

In these cases skilful questioning is used to establish what the client wants to discuss.

Once the session focus is established, **a goal is set for the session**. This is usually identified as the client gaining **deeper understanding** of something or creating an **action plan** to overcome a challenge.

Stage 4: Exploration

Here the client **considers their situation in depth**. This discussion falls into two areas:

1 Realities

* Details of the situation.
* Solutions the client has already attempted.
* Obstacles the client is experiencing.
* The way the client feels and thinks about the situation.
* The client's expectations for the future.

2 Solutions

* Possible solutions to the challenge(s) in question.

Exploration begins with the client explaining the realities of their current situation. Within this discussion they may identify possible solutions. Whether they do or not, the coach will prompt them to seek further possible solutions once they have fully explored the realities.

Stage 5: Creating a plan

Once the realities and solutions have been fully explored, the client is encouraged to use the insight they have gained to create a **realistic plan** and move forward with their challenge.

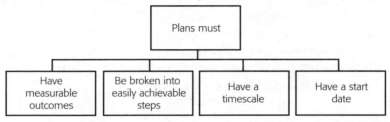

The coach also needs to ensure that the client is fully committed to the plan.

Occasionally a plan is unnecessary because the exploration leads the client to gain understanding that dispels their challenge altogether.

The flow of the process

Within the coaching process there is usually movement back and forth between:

* **Exploration and planning**: when the client considers which solution(s) to implement.
* **Session focus and exploration or planning**: when the client identifies something that leads them to reconsider the goal for the session.

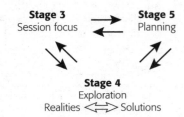

Stage 3 Session focus

Stage 5 Planning

Stage 4 Exploration
Realities ⟺ Solutions

Although the coaching process may seem complex, it is the natural flow of a conversation whereby one person assists another to find solutions or understanding of a situation

CASE STUDY

When Hari finished life coach training he was daunted by the prospect of coaching a real client. However, he quickly became comfortable by ensuring that he prepared well for each session and noted down, in the margin of his notepad, stages 2–5 of the coaching process as:

* reviewing
* session focus
* exploration: realities/solutions
* planning.

This reminded him where he was in the flow of the conversation and to work appropriately.

9 Key coaching skills

The two key skills used by a life coach are **listening** and **questioning**. However, as well as being essential to being a life coach, having good listening and questioning skills can be a huge asset in everyday life.

Skilful use of listening and questioning facilitates full and proper exploration and understanding of a coaching conversation and helps build strong rapport

Good **listening** skills include:

* developing and using the qualities of a good listener
* understanding and using different levels of listening.

Good **questioning** skills include:

* understanding and using different styles of questioning
* understanding and using open and closed questions.

We have two ears and one mouth, so we can hear twice as much as we say.

English saying

Listening qualities

Seven qualities of a good listener that are employed by a coach are:

1 Immediacy

Keeping up with the conversation and paying full attention to it.

2 Seeking clarification

When a good listener does not understand what the speaker is saying, or when the speaker is vague or confused, they seek further explanation. This enables both parties to be clear about what is really being said.

3 Giving feedback

By reflecting back to the speaker what they hear, the listener can:

* check that they have understood what is being said
* act as a mirror that allows the speaker to have greater clarity on what he or she is saying.

4 Genuineness

A good listener takes genuine interest in whatever is said.

5 Empathy

This means being able to imagine yourself in the speaker's place and understand their perspective. It does not necessarily mean that you personally feel the same way as they feel about what they are telling you.

6 Respect

A respectful listener allows the speaker to express and explain their views and beliefs.

7 Curiosity

A good listener becomes curious about what the speaker is telling them.

Levels of listening

There are three levels on which people listen:

Level 1: Internal listening

Here the conversation is listened to and interpreted in terms of how it impacts on the listener.

Because the entire focus of a coaching conversation is on the client, the coach only listens on level 1 when they are dealing with practicalities, such as booking the next appointment.

Level 2: Focused listening

This is the level that the coach usually listens at within the coaching session. Their attention is totally focused on what the speaker says, what they don't say and the speaker's body language, tone and emotion.

Level 3: Global listening

At this level the coach is not aware of exactly what signals they are picking up, but intuitively understands the unspoken messages the client is sending. This may seem rather intangible, but, being aware of the existence of global listening, enables the coach to have the confidence to go with gut feeling.

While listening on levels 2 and 3 and employing the skills of a good listener, the coach must also:

* give encouragement both verbally and non-verbally
* acknowledge success and give praise.

Styles of questioning

The way we ask a question influences the information we receive.

Coaches never ask leading questions.

| Leading questions imply the answer in the question | This suggests the 'right' answer to the listener ... | ... and puts pressure on the listener to agree with the speaker |

For example:

| You don't really think you're smart enough to get that job, do you? | → | The listener questions whether he or she is smart enough | → | The listener may not apply for the job, because he or she believes the speaker or is concerned the speaker is right |

Coaches do ask:

☑ **Questions that focus attention on:**
  a the current situation
  b the client's current experiences and interpretation of those experiences.
☑ **Questions that challenge** assumptions that clients are making or thinking patterns that they are unquestioningly following.
☑ **Questions that clarify:**
  a exactly what the client is saying
  b by asking for greater detail when the coach thinks that they hear an underlying pattern or something significant.
☑ **Questions that tie things down** when the client is being evasive.

Asking the right questions
is vital to good coaching

Open and closed questions

When we talk about a question being open or closed this refers to the amount of information the question seeks.

Closed questions ask for specific information such as:

* 'Yes' or 'No'
* a correct answer
* a decision.

Open questions invite respondents to interpret the level of detail they give in response.

Coaches choose to use open or closed questions depending on the type of information they require.

An open question

Encourages the client to expand on what they are saying

A closed question

Ties the client down

Bullet Guide: Life Coaching

CASE STUDY

Student life coach Ali seemed incapable of coaching his practice partners without interrupting in order to:

* agree with them
* give his opinion
* share his experience
* offer solutions.

It wasn't until his mentor gave him two practice sessions, one in which she acted as a coach who kept interrupting him and one in which she did not, that he realized:

1 how unhelpful he was being
2 the real difference between level 1 and level 2 listening
3 that asking questions helped the client find solutions, which Ali would never have thought of, that were much more suitable.

10 The coaching conversation

The role of a life coach is to facilitate clients to identify and make **changes** that **release their true potential** in order to live **happier, more successful lives**. The way the coach behaves is crucial to the success of the coaching relationship.

A coach always respects each client's individual needs, limitations and boundaries

As well as using strong listening and questioning skills, a coach achieves the unique synergy that is created within a coaching session by:

* giving the client space to explore their agenda
* respecting the client
* raising limiting thinking in the client's awareness
* being totally non-directive and non-judgemental
* diligently observing the client's language and thinking patterns
* encouraging creativity and full exploration of the client's agenda.

We cannot teach people anything; we can only help them discover it for themselves.

Galileo

What coaches do

Unlike an ordinary two-way conversation, in which each speaker takes it in turn to say a few words or sentences, the coach enables the client to speak for the majority of time. This **provides space for the client to explore their agenda**.

The coach listens intently until the client chooses to stop speaking

The coach allows approximately **3 seconds silence**

The client has space to add afterthoughts, which can sometimes be the most important part of the discussion

A life coach identifies unhelpful thinking patterns, negativity, assumptions and beliefs and raises them in the client's awareness.

In order to fully support the client it is crucial that a life coach **consistently honours and respects** the client's:

* beliefs
* values
* goals
* limitations
* individuality
* personal boundaries
* ambitions.

Good communication is essential to successful coaching. A life coach therefore needs to ensure that they **build a strong and natural rapport** with each client.

What coaches don't do

Coaching addresses only the present and the future. If the coaching process unearths unresolved issues, **the coach does not attempt to counsel** but supports the client to identify the best way to move forwards from this discovery.

The coach never **judges** the client's agenda, views or beliefs and never allows their own personal viewpoint to influence their communication or attitude towards a client.

A coach should not continue to work with a client if they find themselves unable to fully fulfil their role as coach.

Clients **always** create their own plans and make their own judgements. **Ownership is vital** if clients are to explore their thinking fully and accurately and create truly rewarding goals. The life coach must therefore be completely **non-directive**.

Coaches never:

✗ *tell*
✗ *train*
✗ *teach*
✗ *advise.*

If a coach has a suggestion they believe may benefit a client, they must first ask, 'May I make a suggestion?'. If the client is amenable, the coach can then make the suggestion. However, the coach must remain detached from the suggestion and not attempt to influence the client to act on it.

Sensory processing

We take information about the world in through all five of our senses. However, most of us have a **preferred sense**, which we rely on more strongly both to experience the world and to internally process it. This is usually seeing, hearing or feeling.

The language the client uses allows a coach to recognize the client's preferred sense. Coaches can then use this awareness to:

* modify their own language to match the client's language and build stronger rapport with the client
* enable the client to use their sensory preference to their advantage.

Preference	Typical words used	Typical types of phrases used	Motivated more strongly by
Visual (seeing)	Clear, focus, outlook, show reveal, look	'I see what you mean' 'I can't picture it' 'I'm in the dark on that one'	Visualization Treasure maps Creating a timeline
Aural (hearing)	Say, sound, harmony, ask, voice, tune	'I hear what you're saying' 'He's not speaking my language' 'It's not ringing any bells with me'	Quotes Music Affirmations
Kinaesthetic (feelings and emotions)	Handle, touch, impress, grab, move, feel	'Feels good to me' 'I can't get to grips with it' 'You've lost me'	Taking action Celebration Praise

Brainstorming

A coach encourages each client to be creative and find new solutions to the challenges they face. This is often done when seeking solutions in the **exploration stage** of the coaching process. Brainstorming can be a useful technique to use here.

Effective brainstorming

The coach should encourage the client to:

* come up with as many answers as they can think of
* refrain from judging any one idea, but simply keep looking for more
* aim to create as long a list as possible
* come up with three more ideas once they think they can't come up with any more.

CASE STUDY

Jessica loved being a life coach. She marvelled at how sometimes she would ask only a few questions and her clients would practically coach themselves as she remained almost silent, simply prompting or giving occasional praise, feedback and acknowledgement. Jessica also felt exhilarated by the creative and unexpected solutions her clients found when she simply:

* remained focused on them
* became curious
* believed in them
* acted non-judgmentally
* gave no suggestions or advice
* encouraged them.

Further reading

Effective Coaching: Lessons from the Coach's Coach by M. Downey (Texere Publishing, 2003).

Feel the Fear and do it Anyway by S. Jeffers (Arrow, 2011).

Time to Think: Listening to Ignite the Human Mind by N. Kline (Cassell, 1998).

The Life Coaching Handbook: Everything You Need to Be an Effective Life Coach by C. Martin (Crown House Publishing, 2001).

Coaching with NLP: How to be a Master Coach by J. O'Conner (Element, 2004).

The Coaching Manual: the Definitive Guide to the Process, Principles and Skills of Personal Coaching by J. Starr (Prentice Hall Business, 2010).

My own book, *Coach Yourself to Writing Success*, is published by Hodder, Teach Yourself (2011). It is based on my experience of using life-coaching techniques to coach aspiring and professional writers to overcome both personal and writing challenges, such as writers' block, procrastination, motivation and lack of time.

At the time of this book going to press, life coaching is not a fully regulated profession with one overseeing body or set of standards. It is therefore prudent if you wish to train to become a life coach to research training providers thoroughly. Furthermore, many coaches specialize in working with particular types of clients. If you wish to employ a life coach, good research should identify coaches who will be best suited to your needs. Competent life coaches should always be happy to answer enquiries from prospective clients about their training and/or professional experience.